TRAILS OF STARDUST

Poems of Inspiration and Insight

by

Donna Huber Miesbach

To

Celize

With love + gratitude

Donna

TRAILS OF STARDUST

Poems of Inspiration and Insight

by

Donna Huber Miesbach

A Pennyworth Book

Published October, 2002

A number of the poems published here first appeared in somewhat different form, individually and collectively, in other publications such as those listed below:
Chicken Soup for the Teenage Soul II, *Unity* Magazine, *Daily Word, The Poet* Magazine, Unity Books, *Tools for Teens*™ - *A Course in Life Skills for People on the Growing Edge, Gleanings - A Bi-Monthly Discussion of Life Issues*™. © Abingdon Press

Cover art: Becky Enholm
Final edit: William G. Carrington

Library of Congress Control Number: 2002114075
Miesbach, Donna H., 1934-
         Trails Of Stardust

ISBN 1-888701-16-1 (paper)

Ah, Gentle Mary, available in anthem format from Abingdon Press.
Oh Centered Candle, available in anthem format July, 2003.
© 2002 Abingdon Press; admin. by
The Copyright Co., Nashville, TN

Copies of this book may be obtained from Pennyworth Press, *pennyworthpress@aol.com*, or from Miesbach Associates, 2805 So. 161st Plaza, Omaha, NB 68130

Phone orders and information requests should be directed to (402) 330-2474.

TRACES OF THE INFINITE

Was that a shooting star I saw
There on the horizon
Or a momentary glimpse
Of the sweeping hand of God,
Leaving in its wake
Traces of the infinite?

Sometimes I think I see
That same hand at work
Within our lives
When doubt grows into faith
And blossoms into love,
Leaving trails of stardust
In our hearts.

LISTEN!

Listen, mortal man!
Do you hear?
The worlds are softly humming
In their spheres,
The universe is swinging to a
Rhythm undefined,
The angels singing strains
Not yet heard by human kind.

Oh listen, mortals,
Do you hear?
The heartstrings gently now
Are being plucked,
The soul set to shimmering
By chords that have been struck.

So quiet now -
Be oh so still -
Attune your inner ear
And you will hear within your heart
The music of the spheres.

PERHAPS!

We are "earthbound" now
But what of then?
When the lesson's learned,
The bloom's grown full,
What is it then that I will be?
What turn within my destiny
Will come as I am born anew?
Something I've not thought of yet
But which awaits as, step on step,
The thought is formed -
The thrust is given -
And there emerges
Fresh and new
The thing that I've been growing to!

Perhaps the process never ends!
Perhaps each finish just begins
Another newer, grander phase
As God reveals in wondrous ways
The fullness of His Love!
Perhaps!

THE PEACE OF EVENING

I feel the peace of evening
Approach on quiet feet,
Silent as a breath of air -
Just as lovely, just as sweet.

'Tis only in the twilight
I can hear its silent step,
Only in the quietness
Feel its gentle breath

As, like a white descending dove
Or unseen angel's wings,
I feel the peace of evening
And the beauty that it brings.

BY WHAT GRACE

Who is it that wanders thus
Through flower-strewn fields
And star-lit skies?
What silent majesty doth stand
In ageless peaks
Where grandeur hides
In towering trees
That watch the ages
Come and go?
Whose mighty power
Imbues the seas
With universes yet unknown
By mortal man?
By what grace does intellect
Allow the soul to ponder thus,
Or love to soar
And soaring, free
The sacred soul
From mortal dust?

A PRAYER

A prayer, oh Lord, I make today
Not just that you would guide my way,
Nor that you'd guard my every word
Or even that my thoughts be heard,
But that I might a blessing be
To all whose lives are touched by me
And that somehow you'd gently bless
All those on whom my vision rests.

TRACINGS

The morning hush lies all around
Like dew upon the grass
Whispering its secrets
To any who might pass.

Birdsong breaks the silence -
Feathered hearts cannot be still -
Rejoicing in the beauty
Of their Creator's will.

Sunlight streaming through the trees
On children now at play
Bringing faithful witness
To yet another day.

Tracings -
Like a finger
Writing in the sand -
Bearing silent evidence
Of the Almighty Hand.

SOMEWHERE, SOMEHOW

There is a hush
About this hour
That words cannot convey,
A holiness
That seems to want
To sanctify the day
And all the many
Busy things
Just seem to slip away.
Somewhere, somehow
A little child
Must have stopped to pray.

RHAPSODY

Iridescent dew drops
sitting on a stem
fragile womb of color
a rhapsody within
for just the briefest moment
everything is still
silence in my spirit
peace upon the hill

WHAT SWEET JOY IS THIS

Tell me now -
Can you embrace the pain
Of mortal longing,
Can you welcome it
This day, this hour?
Can you run with it
And chase it wildly
So as not to miss
One moment of its
Exquisite suffering?

What sweet joy is this
That moves beyond all sorrow
Until even the pain
Is changed
To dancing?

FAITH'S OWN PRISM

Far as the eye can see
Are implications of eternity.
Immediate impressions lend
Unknowing vistas to the
Ever-watchful inner eye
That sees through
Faith's own prism
Worlds yet undefined.
Crystal clear is
The refraction which,
When captured in the inner eye,
Is reflected just as truly
As the sunlight gently caught
In morning's dew.

RIVERS

I wonder what the rivers are
That flow within my mind.
Are they peace and beauty,
Joy and love -
I wonder what I'd find
Were I to go a-walking there
As through a shady wood.
Would I find rest and comfort
Just as a traveler should?
I'd like to be a quiet place
For weary souls to rest.
I'd like to be a peaceful place
To soothe each wand'ring guest.

INNER JOURNEY

I would not follow those
Long and distant roads leading
Off to the horizon
For there are roads I
Have not yet explored
That lead within,
And something tells me -
Is it my inner self I hear? -
That there is greater treasure
Hidden in the secret recesses
Of my being
Than I could ever hope to find
In other lands.

THE KEY

Ah, my child -
<u>Mind</u> is the key
For it is here
that you live,
It is here
that you accept or reject
your good,
It is here
that you initiate
change.
Whatever you would be,
You must be it first
in your mind.
Whatever you would achieve,
You must achieve it first
in your mind.
You see, my child -
Mind is, You are, I AM -
We are one being -
One Mind -
And all the rest
is but a
reflection.

SIGNATURES

Tiny pebbles in the stream
Made silky smooth by
Endless drops of liquid life
Much as the flow of time
Works on the mortal soul
Washing away the juts and crags
'Til only the core remains.
Pebbles, souls, it's all the same -
Signatures of time.

BE STILL

Be still, my soul
and question not
The unseen hand
that wrought the plot
That brought you to
this time and place,
For all your doubts
will not erase
The things that made you
what you are
And brought you to
this very hour,
So do not strain
or question why.
The stars are in their place -
and so am I!

THE WILLOW TREE

I am like the willow tree
Flowing with the wind,
For I know not when life's pathway
May take a sudden bend
Or what unexpected stresses
May require of me,
And so I find it wisest
Just to supple be
That I may bend but never break,
Just like the willow tree.

HOW?

How could we strengthen courage
If there were no challenges to meet?
How could we be unselfish
If no evil to defeat?
How could we strive for service
If all was just and fair,
Or cling to hope and trust
If no doubts were anywhere?
How could our faith begin to grow
If we could not aspire
To the ideals wrought by truth
If there was nothing higher?
Would pleasure really satisfy
Had we never known some pain,
Or love of truth inspire us
If there was naught to gain?
How could we choose to love Him
If no choice was ours to make?
How could we choose to serve Him
And our willfulness forsake
If we did not have the freedom
To choose the higher will
And in the act of choosing
Our destiny fulfill!

WOULD YOU?

What is this love
You say you are seeking?
Do you want it enough
To climb the high mountains?
Would you endure the
Cracked and parched lips
Of desert lands?
How great is the longing
You say you have
Inside you?
If the price were
All of this
Would you render it
Gladly
To taste one sweet moment
Of bliss?

THE PRIZE IS NOT THE WINNING

You have to swim the waters
To reach the other side.
You have to trust the Lord
To in His peace abide.

You have to face the conflict
If ever you'd be free
To rise above all doubt and fear
And claim your victory

For the prize is not the winning
When at last the struggle's o'er
But more, the valiant effort
That brought you to the shore!

WHEN YOU CAN

My child, when you can
be at peace
in the midst of unrest,
be loving
in the midst of anger,
be calm
where there is fear,
be whole
where there is sickness,
When you can
overflow
in the threat of lack,
<u>know</u>
when faced with doubt,
Then, my child,
you shall have overcome
the world.

THE SURER TRAIL

If only we could understand,
When we perchance may fail,
That lessons learned might ne'er have come
Had we not sought so high a trail
For it is when, with all our heart,
We reach for something higher
We may come close, but not quite reach,
The good that we aspire
Yet much is gained and nothing's lost,
For failure's quick to teach
Us how to climb the surer trail
As toward the heights we reach!

AS A SEED

Lord, let me be as
One small seed
That questions not, but
Sends its roots into the
Dark from whence it
Neither sees nor knows
The way its needs shall be
Fulfilled.

Lord, let me trust as
This small seed
So I, too, may
Reach into the dark
And find You there.

THE EDGE OF DARKNESS

Were it not for earth's dark shadow
That turns the day to night
The time would never come when I
Could welcome morning's light.
So, too, when griefs around me spread,
The eye breaks forth a tear,
My soul then most keenly knows
That God is ever near.
So all life's tests and trials
Cast their shadows on the day
But their very edge of darkness
More clearly shows the way,
For light would never seem as bright,
Its jewel quite so fair,
Had there never been a shadow
To frame it in somewhere.

WE MUST BE MINDFUL

I think the angels
must have wondered
when they heard
that great explosion -
They did not know
that God was
making stars.

So with us -
when chaos seems apparent -
we must be mindful
that Good is being formed
and even now is destined
to occur.

THIS NEW DAY

Dear Lord, this day so fresh and new,
Untouched by anyone but You,
Comes on silent little feet,
All humble, still and meek.
Help me to be as this day is
And, loving Thee, may I so live
That my whole world might somehow be
Blessed by Thee eternally.

GRACE

Grace passed by this afternoon
On wings transparent-white
And had I not been watching
I'd have missed its lovely flight
For not a sound did it be-stir
As it so quietly
Came floating by on summer breeze
For all who cared to see.

How often in our daily lives
Has Grace come floating by
But we, with all our hurrying,
Quite missed the passer-by?
It makes me think that angels
Might just as present be
If we'd but slow our busy pace
And take the time to see!

WHEN DREAMS COME CALLING

Sometimes
In the middle of the night
A dream comes peeking in
Tip-toeing around the fringes
Of your half-awakened mind
Looking to see
If there are any takers -
Is anyone at home
Or shall I find another?

Sometimes in the middle
Of your dreams
A silver thread of
Moonlight
Breaks through the
Soft velvet of the night
Just long enough to leave
The faint traces of a kiss
On your half-awakened eyes.

Sometimes.

DARLING LITTLE DAYSPRITE

Happy little child
Dancing in the sunlight
Was it so very different
Where you were before?

Who were your companions
Playing in the meadow
Fancy free and happy
Your spirits light and gay?

What is that bit of sparkle
That stardust on the edges
Could it be the wings
You forgot to put away?

Perhaps you're here in daytime
And over there when sleeping
Perhaps you're in this world
And also in the next.

Oh darling little daysprite
Heartbeam of my spirit
Whisper now your secret
That I may join your play!

GLORY SPRINGETH WITH THE DAWN

The sky is but a patch-work quilt
Of pink and white and blue
Reflected on the meadow grass
All lightly wet with dew.

The sun, the herald of the morn,
Resumes its royal place
While breeze and birdsong, tree and flower
Greet the welcome face

For glory springeth with the dawn
Its visage to portray
And all earth wakes to welcome
The birth of the new day,

But I, a humble witness
As it plays its mighty role,
Can only stand in awe to see
It rising in my soul.

A TOUCH OF GRACE

The air seems so much sweeter now
The love feels much more deep somehow
The smiles, the hugs, the warm embrace
Are rather like a touch of grace,
And all the world's many faces
Whisper of those other places
Where I first breathed this fragrant air
Within the depths of quiet prayer.

ONLY LOVE

Let there be only love
In this, my life,
For then there will be only love
In this, my world,
So that no matter
What I see
It will all be love to me
And, too, no matter
Who I meet
It will still be love I greet.
Oh may the day never begin
Without the simple prayer within -
Let there be only love
In this, my life!

THE GIFT

My being is so full of the
pure, crystalline life of God
that I think if you were to
tap my shoulder,
it would ring like a bell!
Joy is its keynote,
and its tonic chord is love.
The cells that compose it
fairly dance with joy as they
go about their perfect work
free of stress and strain,
moving easily within their
sphere of perfection
doing that which is theirs to do.
What a beautiful
symphony of life!
No wonder my soul is singing
and my very spirit is
effervescing with the
sheer joy of being.
So this is life!
And to think
the gift is eternal ...

MIRRORS

Last night I rode the lightning
Across the midnight sky,
I saw the mighty thunderheads
And heard the heavens cry,
I watched the many raindrops
As they made their way to earth
Bringing verdant life to all
That waited Spring's new birth.
But now the storm is over,
The lightning's gone to bed
And so I don a radiant robe
Of morning light instead.
I see my own reflection
In tiny, dewy flowers
And watch the children come to play
In happy morning hours.
The robin singing merrily
Speaks of my presence there
But most of all I hear my name
Within the heart at prayer.

ANOTHER GARDEN

It is Spring-time in the
Garden of my soul -
New currents of the spirit
Are wafting through me now.
Light I have not seen before
Has come into my sight
And all around me
Blossoms are
That came up in the night.
My soul's a-bloom!
And the fragrance it exudes
Speaks of another Garden where
I walk and talk enfolded
In the quietness of prayer

INNER WINGS

The coastal squadron, flying low,
A mighty shadow makes
As feathered wings, extended wide,
The mighty current takes.
So might I, too, with inner wings
Sail my unseen sea
And find at last, at journey's end,
That it was naught but Thee.

THE RISING TIDE

East of the silver moon
Is a September sky
Where rivulets of joy
Meet the rising tide
Of love that cannot be contained
That is ever freely sent
And all earth stands on tiptoe
To see the great event.

ONLY IN THE STILLNESS

Only in the stillness
can the dew descend
As in the morning's coolness
the heat comes to an end;
Only in the quiet
can the spirit be renewed
And filled with peace that's only found
in inner solitude.

In each moment's newness
fresh thoughts somehow are formed,
In our heart's own yearning
our dreams become re-born,
For ever in the silence
the inner work is done
And ever in our spirit
the battle first is won!

FINCHES AND FIRELIGHT

Lilacs and lilies
Sunset's rich glow
Colors cascading
Like new-fallen snow,
Finches and firelight
Gracing my room
All but ignoring
The emerald moon

THE DAFFODIL

The daffodil's a-quiver
With the newness of its blossoming.
Tender as the fresh-born fawn
It glistens in the sun.
The joy it feels becomes my own
For I am blooming, too,
And through this kindred Spirit
We both are born anew!

I'LL BE SURE TO LET YOU KNOW

What is more important
Than sunning on the bough?
I don't know
But if I find out
I'll be sure to let you know -
Someday -
When the silence is worth
The breaking.

SIMPLY IN BEING

Nature's creations,
Though silent they be,
Speak to us all
Eloquently.
No voice have they
Nor tongue nor pen.
Simply in being
Their message is given.
Oh what a lesson
To those who have tongues
That simply in being
The Spirit hath sung!

THE BUTTERFLY

I've caught the sunlight in my wings
and move with easy and grace
for spirit is my medium
And earth my dwelling place,
But once I crawled on tiny feet
Amid the dust of earth
Until at last I turned within
and found my own new birth.
'Tis through the chrysalis of prayer
My soul now freely sings
For when at last I did emerge
Christ Light was captured in my wings.
Yes, I am ever spirit's child,
All grace and ease commanding.
Born within a moment
Of quiet understanding.

FOOTPRINTS

Oh Lord, this day so fresh and new
Glistens in the morning dew
And every footstep that I take
Doth a new impression make.
Oh, let my footsteps gentle be,
Each loving act my alms to Thee,
And may each little thing I do
Become a hymn of praise to you.
Oh, may the imprints that I make
A trail to Thee leave in my wake,
A pathway carved by Love Divine
From footprints in the sands of time.

THE GOLDEN HOUR

Quiet as the morning dew
The sunlight creeps into my room,
Waking me with loving thoughts
For day is starting soon.
'Tis time to go within
Into the garden of my soul,
To touch the inner springs of life
And know that I am whole.
'Tis time to hear the message
That in the silence speaks,
To feast on hidden manna
That my inner spirit seeks.
It is the time of silence,
The golden, sacred hour
Where Spirit speaks to Spirit's own
And there is touched with power.

IMPRINTS

When I resolve into the essence
Which I most truly am
I feel a deep connection
With every living thing,
For That which most imbues me
With my identity
Is somehow in the other, too,
So that when I look around
I see myself - reflected.
Hidden in this union
Is the wonderful discovery
That if indeed the angels
May have wings -
Then so do I.
And if the essence of a flower
Drifts out on gentle breeze -
Then so do I.
And if the midnight sky
Is radiant with light -
Then so am I.
And if the silent mystery
Somehow becomes revealed
In tiny dew drops fair -
Then so am I,
For every lovely thing
Manifests the essence
That I am.
Oh beware, my soul, beware,
And move with gentle heart
Throughout this mystic veil
For if Love has left its imprint here -
Then so have I!

BREAKERS

The tides wash in upon my shore
Where lonely breakers meet,
Where solitary thoughts a-drift
Float gently to my feet.

The timeless pull of endlessness
Draws me beyond the reef
Where in the quiet otherness
The silent secrets keep.

How could I never heed the call?
How could I wait too long?
For this same inner longing
Is the mystic song

That ever rings within my heart,
That whispers night and day
Of love that breaks upon my shore
And washes cares away!

JEWELS

There are regions of my mind
where I've never gone before,
and thoughts I've not yet thought of
that beckon from the door
I've come to know as consciousness -
the inner realm of "me" -
and what I do about them
is purely up to me,
so I shall go exploring
and the inner steeps I'll climb
so I may find the jewels
that lay hidden in my mind.

SILHOUETTES

The haze has settled on the hills
As evening's dusk lays bare
The ridges that betray their form
Encircling everywhere.
Only the crest can still be seen,
Only the outline there
As silently they melt in the dark,
Awaiting the morning air.
Oft in the twilight when all of my thoughts
Have settled like dusk on the hills
And all of my cares have dissolved into peace
My being once again thrills
To think of the time when all was new,
When the concept, pure and fair,
Was easily seen, like the hills at dusk,
And peace reigned everywhere.
Then I realize once more that nothing has changed -
That my spirit is still fresh and whole -
As here in the dusk I sense once again
The silhouette of my soul.

REFLECTIONS

In the glow of evening
Thoughts, like fine, gossamer filaments,
Weave their way across my mind.
The deep stillness at day's end
Speaks in the utter silence
Of the allness of Being
Which ever folds me 'round.
The rosy glow of Love spreads like a blanket
Across my world while
The golden sheen of life still lights my day.
And here am I,
immersed,
at peace,
filled with the
Beauty and the stillness
Until I, too, fade into evening's rest,
A prelude to morning's renewal of my
Eternal tryst with God.
Now I see morning's glow upon the horizon
And know it is but a reflection
Of the Light rising within me,
A silent proclamation of the
Eternal Presence within this body
That is more "me" than "I" am,
And as I study the beauty and majesty
That presents itself before me,
I know that this, too, is mine
As the inner Light takes on full sway.
No, not mine but Thine, and yet
It has Its Being within me
And therein lies the Truth of my existence.

OH CENTERED CANDLE

Oh centered candle, may I by thy light
Move my heart steadfastly toward thee.
Oh may thy light a beacon be
That I might find my life in thee.

When, in the dawn of each new day,
Thy light breaks forth upon my soul
So may I seek to find my way
And stumble not upon the shoal

That ever lurks near trembling feet
Which, pressing forth to grace the dawn,
Move with haste thy light to greet
While night's last tendrils linger on.

Oh gentle light, thou art my joy.
My every waking hour yearns for thee
Causing all effort to employ
That I might now more constant be.

Oh centered candle, lead me on
That I may rest my soul in thee
So when at last I reach the dawn
My spirit may be truly free.

WHERE THE ANGELS SING

When I have reached my highest heights
And plumbed my deepest deeps,
When I can see the brightest Truth
That in my spirit keeps,
When I have touched the Light within
And felt its warming ray
And gone beyond the realm of time
Where there is night and day,
When I have found the substance pure
In every lovely thing,
I've gone beyond the edge of self
To where the angels sing!

BE STILL, MY SOUL, AND LISTEN!

Be still, my soul, and listen!
Do you hear the silent deeps?
Do you hear the inner stillness
That eternal secrets keep?

Can you hear the gentle moonlight,
Can you hear the break of day?
Can you hear the planets singing
As they spin upon their way?

Can you sense the thought of birdsong,
The thought of tranquil peace
That settles in the evening
Bringing day its sweet release?

Oh be still, my soul, and listen
To the message of the deeps
For there, within your heart-song,
Eternal secrets keep!

DID YOU?

Did you hear God whisper
When the morning came?
His voice was in the sunrise -
I heard Him call my name
Again, within the buttercup
All glistening with dew,
In it's tiny little blossom
All fresh and sweet and new
I saw Him smile,
I felt His love -
And when the gentle
Mourning dove
Took flight on feathered wing
I felt God's song stir in my heart -
Oh yes, I heard Him sing!
And there were bells that
No one rang
That echoed in my ear -
As morning's hush drew all around
I felt my Father near.
Oh, did you hear God whisper?
Did you hear Him sing?
He spoke to me this morning
In every lovely thing!

I LOVE THE JOY

I love these hills,
this verdant earth
The rolling waves,
exploding surf
I love the way
the morning light
Is captured in the
seagull's flight
I love the joy,
the power, the day
The dancing foam,
the sea at play
I love the life,
the scented air
The gods at play
are everywhere.

CONSTELLATIONS

Oh Beings of the Cosmos,
What great body clothes you?
I see your constellations,
Distant reminders of your presence,
But who are you
And how did you chance
To be my guide?

The cosmos within me
Hears your faint and subtle calling
A light shared between us
A flickering message
Of hope and love.
The stars are shining -
Yours and mine -
And who is to say
If they are different?

TIME TO GO HOME

The tendrils of light still left in the sky
Have painted a radiant dome
That speaks to my soul of peace and of love
And I know it is time to go home.

Time to return to my Father's work,
To feast on His living Word,
To listen again to His lingering voice
That my soul long ago heard.

Oh the days go by and the years somehow flee
As my footsteps wander and roam,
But deep in my heart I can hear Him call
And I know it is time to go home.

TOO SOON

Reluctantly
The trees turn brown,
Too soon the leaves
Come floating down,
Too soon the frost
Its visit pays,
Too quick the sun
Finds shortened rays.

The day that once was
Mild and fair,
The breeze that once
Brought summer's air,
All have softly
Crept away -
"Too soon, too soon," they
Seem to say.

It is no less with you or me
As fate or sometimes
Destiny
Comes creeping over
Timeless hills
While in our hearts
The message spills
Until we can
Deny no more
What really we had
Known before -
Too soon, we stand
Before the door.

IF E'ER A CHILD

A Mother's heartache
Is such a poignant thing -
Her depth of love
Untold mercies brings
And every soft and
Gentle tear
Makes a sound
That angels hear.
If e'er a child did
Blossom fair,
Somewhere a Mother
Must have cared.

A MOTHER'S HANDS

There is nothing so dear
As a Mother's hands -
Gentle, sweet and kind -
Cool and soft on a
Fevered brow
With comfort and love entwined.
Ah, how the memories
Flood from the past
Of many a by-gone day
When I think of the touch
Of my dear Mother's hands
And the cares that they
Smoothed away.

AH, GENTLE MARY

Ah, gentle Mary,
Did the breeze caress you
As in the musty light you bore
The gift that still resides
In faith-filled hearts?

Ah, gentle Mary,
Did the earthy stable sounds
Offer the first lullaby
To soothe your little child so new
Resting in the hay?

Ah, gentle Mary,
How you must have pondered
The future so uncertain.
How could you have known then
The road that lay before him
As you wrapped him in your prayers
So gentle, Mary. Ah...

PASSING THROUGH

Death is but a broadening of sight,
A moving out of darkness into light,
And as your essence thus becomes refined
So also do you move into the heart of mind.
It is a moment, then, of sweet release
Imbued with such transcending peace
That were it seen like this before
The soul would welcome such a door
And gently pass its being through
Into the realm of life anew.

NO LONGER THAN A GLANCE

Dearest Heart,
I would not leave thee.
Never would I choose
To have our life-paths part.
The price of age sometimes
Is more than I can bear
And yet, my love, I know
That when we leave this earthly plane,
It is just a moment, love,
A blink within eternity,
Before we meet again -
No longer than a glance is all
Before I see your face
Upon that joyful other shore
Where, holding out your hand to me,
I help you through the door.

LOOK IN YOUR HEART

Do not weep for me, my child,
For I am free at last
Of all of the encumbrances
That held me in their grasp.
Now my spirit freely soars,
Released from all its pain,
And heights I could not reach before
Now need no stress or strain.
Transcendent joy is mine at last,
Immortal Love my pure repast,
So do not grieve, do not despair -
Look in your heart - I will be there.

THEY ARE THE DREAMS

Where is the child that once was so carefree
Where is the youth that danced with the morn
Where is the spirit that caught the horizon
And gently carried it under her arm?

Where is the Mother who sang to her baby
Where is the woman who stood so forlorn
Watering flowers that grew by the graveside
With tears that flowed from a heart so torn?

Where is the one who walked through the daisies
Who walked in the field all barefoot and free
Where is the one who greeted the sunset
And pondered just what tomorrow might be?

They are still here - No, they have not left you
They are the dance of the spirit at dawn
They are the mirrors that once did reflect you
They are the dreams that awoke with the morn.

THAT STAR IS YOU

These worlds -
These distant stars -
Spinning out of nothingness -
That, too, is you, dear soul,
For out of the heart of infinity,
Out of the metamorphic deep
A call was heard -
A soul was formed -
And there you came
All shining, new.

Oh yes, that star
Is you, oh soul,
And the darkness of this world
Is but a backdrop
For the eternal splendor
Of that glint of Truth,
That spark of Life,
That bit of Love
That came spinning
Out of infinity
Toward some grander destiny,
Leaving trails of stardust
In its wake.

ALWAYS YOU WERE THERE

When was it I first met you,
When I saw you face to face -
When I tasted of your presence,
When you touched me with your grace?
Was it standing here upon the shore
Or from mountain's lofty view?
In all the sunsets of my days
Weren't you there then, too?
I saw you in my new-born babe
Gazing out through infant eyes -
How different it must have seemed to you
Compared to Paradise.
I felt that same pure sweetness
In the touch of parents' hands
And even in my early youth
I seemed to understand
That always I have known you,
Always you were there;
Whether here or pure unbounded space
You were everywhere.

ANOTHER PLACE

There is a place -
another space -
That speaks to my inner ear.
It's far too interior
to have a name,
Too sacred to ever be spoken.

The Spirit there swirls
and curls itself
As it whispers again in my ear
Unfurling before me
infinite truths
That only my soul can hear.

Oh there is a place -
an infinite space -
That only the heart can open
And it whispers my name
like the breath of the wind,
Too sacred to ever be spoken.

TWO DISTANT WORLDS

We live in two distant worlds,
You and I,
And yet we share a common bond
That all the differences
Cannot divide,
And all the years
Or joys or tears
Have not the means
To separate
The bond that makes us one.
Yes, we are not dissolvable
For we have built a span
That long ago began
Within our hearts.

THE SHORE

I stand on the edge of consciousness
where I am not so much myself
as I just simply Am.

In this moment of Peace
I enter into the sea of Pure Being
and am caught up in the
wonder of this Spirit,
so fluid,
so alive,
yet so still and so silent that the
sheer force of it fills me with
feelings that have no words, and
thoughts that have not yet found their
meanings in the depths of my mortal mind.

And yet, in their own
symphony of soundless sound, the
meanings are clear, and the
sounds ring through me with a

clarity and trueness that tells me
that this is the Truth of all Being,
the symphony of my soul,
the harmony of life -
and that even as I return to the
shore of my own personal self, the
Truth I have felt and heard will remain
as an indelible part of my being, and
the songs I will sing will flow out from
these depths where time and again
I will return
to fill the cup,
to refresh and renew the soul,
to be One in that infinite moment
where, alone with my Creator and my God,
all is answered
and all is complete
and there is only
One.

THE FUTURE IS A-BORNING

The butterfly's cocooning
Now that winter's here,
Magically preparing
For yet another year,
While I beside my fire
Cozily do sit,
My mind all vague and fuzzy
And wandering just a bit.
I think we're both cocooning
In this quiet dreamy state;
The future is a-borning
As we both just sit and wait

DOESN'T IT?

Do caterpillars dream about
becoming butterflies?
Do their tiny little feet
want to reach up for the sky?
Why does the youth revere
someone's advancing age
Or the student want to honor
a wise and ancient sage?
Does the inner heart's cocoon
already harbor some
Distant mystic vision
of what it might become?
Do you suppose it's possible
that we just might foresee,
Albeit somewhat dimly,
our metamorphoses?
Perhaps we reach too far
when we attempt to know
Or understand the changes
that we might undergo
But doesn't it seem possible,
if tiny feet can fly,
That the soul might also wonder,
"Why not I?"

WEAVING

I'm weaving on my inner loom
A piece I cannot see
And yet I know the image
Will be uniquely me.

I know not whence the vision
That guides my inner hand
Nor what it is within me
That seems to understand

Just how the pattern should be formed,
Just where the threads should go.
There's Something deep within me
That just seems to know

For threads of every shade and hue
Inextricably
Find their way across my loom
To where they ought to be.

It matters not if dark or light
For each has its own role
As in the silence they portray
The image in my soul.

Oh I'm weaving on an inner loom
A piece I cannot see
And yet the inner image
Will be uniquely me!

IF I WERE A THOUGHT

If I were a thought in the mind of God
I wonder just what I'd be.
Would I be filled with beautiful light,
Drifting, happy and free?

Perhaps I'd be full of colors and hues
Radiant, grand and fair,
Letting all of my colors shine
On everything, everywhere.

Or maybe I'd be a pretty tune
Floating on currents of air
Moving toward a receptive mind
That's waiting for me somewhere.

Of course, I'm just guessing -
I really can't say -
Just how it would actually be,
But this much I know -
If I were God's thought
I'd be happy just to be me!

OH WINGED SPIRIT

Oh winged spirit
Silent and unseen
Force behind all earthly force
All power in between,
This sky is but a single breath
This sea is but a tear
This path a tiny rivulet
This star both far and near.

Oh winged spirit
Life of all,
Come while away the hours
For I would have you dance with me
And sit here, picking flowers.

TEACH ME YOUR SECRET

I love the way you cool my face
With your frothy happy waves
Splashing, playing, tantalizing
One who longs to join you
As you dance in the sunlight
And crash upon the shore,
Tossing yourself into the air
With an abandon that
Could only be born of freedom.
Oh spirit of the waves,
Come teach me your secret
That I, too, might fling myself
Into the universe
And find you there.

THAT WILD AND RECKLESS JOY

Would that I could throw myself
Upon the altar of this life
Like the sea upon the shore
That I might know
That wild and reckless joy
That comes when all
Restraint is gone
And you've given yourself away
Utterly.

ONE THING MORE

If I could
I'd give you wings
To fly your special skies
And courage, too,
I'd send to you
To help your spirit rise...

And breezes fair
And swaying trees
And lovely star-filled nights,
I'd like to give you
All of these
To make your days just right

And then I'd do
Just one thing more -
A prayer of praise I'd send
Because I feel
So very blessed
To have you for my friend.

TO LAUGH IS TO DANCE

How do you say "Good-bye" to the sea,
To the ceaseless, rolling waves -
To the mist and the light
The shore and the life
To the sky and the sea and waves?

How do you say "Hello" to the dawn
To the breaking of morning light -
To the hues and the rays
To the countless days
Cascading beyond human sight?

How do you capture joy in your arms
Or love in your own heart's grasp
Or the laughter and tears
That color the years
And bring all longing to pass?

How do you filter the Truth of it all,
The mystery as yet unseen
That gives birth to the waves
And the light and the sea,
The magic and you and me?

The answer as yet has not offered itself
Yet ever it folds me 'round
As it whispers its message
Deep in my heart
Without ever making a sound.

Oh to have ears that can hear such a voice
That can hear the great cosmic song
For to hear is to laugh
And to laugh is to dance
And to dance is at last to belong.

CHANNELS

Have you ever noticed -
When love is poured out
it deepens?
When joy is shared
it multiplies?
When peace is embodied
it spreads?
When life is blessed
it prospers?
When the spirit is praised
it grows?
When substance is released
it increases?
Do you suppose this is why
we must give
if the Good is to increase?
Perhaps this is why
we are called
channels.

WINGS

My spirit delights
in a new-born thought
As it follows along
and is carried aloft,
Soaring into the
vast unknown,
Hearing it speak
to you alone,
Riding the waves
like currents of air,
Letting it take you
who knows where?
Now I know why
the sea gull sings
For my soul rejoices
when my spirit has wings!

CANYONS

Were I to go exploring
In the canyons of my mind,
Would there be some treasure there?
I wonder what I'd find.
Perhaps a gentle waterfall
Or rare, exotic flowers
Reflecting back my heart-song
As I while away the hours
Following the life-stream
Running ever free,
Discovering the mystery
I've come to know as "me"
While I explore my canyons
Broad and grand and deep
Wherein eternal secrets
Their silent vigil keep.

SEASONS

Wee winter days
With not much light,
Not as much day
As they are night,
A time to rest -
All earth in repose,
Preparing for seasons
That only God knows.

THE MOMENT

The wind's a-gale as the
Drifting snow piles up outside
My door. Nature's creatures are
Hidden in some safe, familiar
Place while all green and growing
Things lay dormant, their summer
Glory but a distant memory in their
Sleeping roots. 'Tis time for
Me, too, to come apart and
Nestle in the cozy warmth of
Blazing hearth, remembering but
Vaguely creation's distant
Conception that long ago gave
Birth to me. Ah, the spark is
Still within me, and if I truly
Listen, I can more feel than
Hear it as it calls me to my
Most inward reach where still
Awaits my Maker for a special
Word with me, kept safe for
Generations, only waiting for the
Moment when I would be
Still.

IN THE DAWN OF WINTER

Dark diamond dreams
In the hush of the night
Seeking the stars,
Seeking the light.

In the dawn of winter
The desert sky unfolds
Spinning an ocean
Of blues and reds and golds.

I SHOULD HAVE KNOWN, LORD

Was that You, Lord?
Was it You my soul was seeking?
Was it You Who touched me in the dark
When I was barely sleeping?

And all the many tears I shed,
When all my being cried,
Are You the One Who came and stood
So gently by my side?

Oh Lord, there were so many times
When, groping in the night,
I felt a hand reach out to me
To take away my fright,

And as the weeks would slip away
That Presence grew and grew.
Oh yes, I should have known, Lord,
That always it was You!

LEGACY

When all is said and done,
My life will feel complete
If I might leave the gift
With all I've chanced to meet

Of knowing they are loved
No matter what transpires
So they might find God's peace
In all that life requires,

For it must surely follow,
No matter what they face,
That they will truly come to know
The beauty of God's grace.

A BLESSING

May your steps be filled with confidence.
May they take you to inspiring places.
May they feed you at your deepest levels.
May they spark your imagination and replenish your spirit.
May they break through all the tangled places in your life, and
Be for you a way of pilgrimage
along the secret mountain of your life,
And as you seek the path to climb it,
May you find it goes within.
May it lead you to peaceful places and healing waters.
May it call you to quiet times that renew and restore
As only true solitude can do.
May it show you that your horizons are really within you,
And may the ancient song of your soul
Adorn the gates through which you enter.
May it reveal the mystic within you.
May it release the laughter that chases away all pain,
And may it take you into that timeless realm
Where words are no longer needed,
Where all the shrines of all your seeking await you.
Yes, someday, in the dusk of evening,
May your footsteps take you
Into your eternal, internal landscape
Where all is as it should be
And all is well.

CREDO

Only to serve Thee
'Tis my soul's one care,
Only to seek Thee
And find Thee there,
Only to love Thee
And feel Thou art near,
That my life may be a song
And my song a prayer.

THE WELL-WORN PATH

I do not write the poem -
It writes itself through me.
With open heart to Spirit's flow
Inwardly I see
The message move
Through hand and pen
Imperceptibly
Until the thought becomes complete
And stillness comes again.

Oft I must go back to find
Just what it was 'twas said,
And as I read it o'er and o'er
New visions stir within my head
That soon will take
The well-worn path
From mind to hand to pen
As in wisdom and in love
God shares a truth again.